SOCIALIST HISTORY SOCIETY

SOCIALIST HISTORY
OCCASIONAL PAPERS SERIES
No 19

KEIR HARDIE IN WEST HAM:
"A CONSTITUENCY WITH A PAST"

W RAYMOND POWELL

2004

Published by the Socialist History Society, 2004

An earlier version of this article was published in *Essex Archaeology and History*, No. 33, 2002

ISBN   0 9537742 6 0

Contents

Introduction

At the end of the nineteenth century, voting patterns in Britain were overwhelmingly dominated by two political parties - the Conservatives and Liberals.

As Private Willis sings in Gilbert and Sullivan's *Iolanthe*:

> Nature always does contrive...
> That every boy and every gal
> That's born into the world alive
> Is either a little Liberal
> Or else a little Conservative.

The situation was not altered by the extension of the franchise. Working men, who received the vote in the towns in 1867 and in the countryside in 1884-85, still voted for the traditional parties. Insofar as any attempt was made to get working men into the House of Commons, it was usually made through the Liberal Party. James Maudsley, the leader of the Lancashire cotton workers, however, like many of his members, was a staunch Conservative and stood as such in the Oldham by-election of 1899.

Although socialism was revived in the last two decades of the nineteenth century, with the foundation of the Social Democratic Federation (1881), the Fabian Society (1884), the Socialist League (1885), the Scottish Labour Party (1888), and the Independent Labour Party (1893), initially it made very little electoral impact.

The first two SDF Parliamentary candidates, Jack Williams in Hampstead and John Fielding in Kennington, in 1885, polled 27 and 32 votes respectively. Although the interest at the time was focussed on the scandal of the SDF accepting "Tory gold" to run the election campaigns, the real lesson was that its electoral support was virtually nil. In Scotland, where the situation was ostensibly more favourable, the formation of the Scottish Labour Party still did not lead to electoral success. In 1892 and 1898, its candidates came in behind the Liberals and Conservatives. Even in West Bradford, with its links to the birth of the ILP, Ben Tillett, as the Parliamentary candidate in 1895, was third in the polls.

It was not in the provinces at all that Labour made its first real breakthrough, but in West Ham South, on the outskirts of London, when James Keir Hardie was elected as the first ever Independent Labour Member of Parliament in 1892. Why and how this occurred is therefore not a matter of mere local interest but one of national importance in British political history. In this detailed study of West Ham politics in the last part of the nineteenth century, W R Powell reveals what occurred and how Labour achieved its first ever take-off.

As he points out, West Ham was, by the 1880s, a booming industrial town with a population approaching 200,000. It was, in some important ways, different from other parts of London, where the older industries had been declining for decades and many of the lower classes were desperately poor, continually on the move and dependent upon casual work and self-employment to keep them and their families out of the workhouse. West Ham and adjoining areas, in contrast, provided a home for newly constructed docks, the Great Eastern Railway Locomotive Works, Beckton Gasworks (in East Ham), shipyards and a whole swathe of dependent engineering, chemical and other industries. Though remote from the coalfields, West Ham had the facilities to unload coal and the railway system to move it around. It sucked in cheap labour from London, the rural hinterland of East Anglia and further afield.

The demand for labour, the absence of pre-existing regulations and structures, and rapid economic growth, created an environment in which new social, industrial, religious and other organisations could be established. The fast growing community was neither hidebound by custom nor threatened by industrial closures. Trade unions, co-operative societies, working men's clubs and political groups came into existence alongside churches, cultural organisations and a variety of social groupings.

Before West Ham South returned James Keir Hardie to Parliament, the area had already served as the seedbed for other pioneering developments in working-class organisation.

After decades of failure to establish a thriving co-operative movement in London, in contrast to the success elsewhere of the model projected by the Rochdale Pioneers, in 1861 Stratford railwaymen founded the Stratford Co-operative Society, which became a major force by the 1880s. It went on to become the nucleus of the London Co-operative Society, established in 1920.

West Ham was also the birthplace of the New Unionism of the 1880s. The successful match girls' struggle of 1888, the epic "dockers' tanner" struggle of 1889 and the achievement of an eight-hour day for the gas workers centred on, or were in the vicinity of, West Ham. Trade union organisation of the unskilled first took off in this area.

Six years after James Keir Hardie's victory in 1898, West Ham became the first borough in Britain ever to return a Labour majority council. This only lasted a year, but it blazed the trail for others and for longer lasting control in West Ham from 1910 onwards.

W R Powell's article traces the political history that led up to the West Ham South Parliamentary election of 1892 and shows how a Labour majority was achieved. Radical Liberals and their organisations made an important contribution to preparing the ground. They had been influenced by trade union struggles, particularly the dockers' tanner strike of 1889 in which many of them had supported the strikers. The Social Democratic Federation and its members were also active in the area. In 1891, Will Thorne, the leader of the gas workers and a SDF member, was elected to the Borough Council and gave Keir Hardie his support. The Stratford Dialectical & Radical Club was a centre of left-wing political activity. Irish voters supported Home Rule for Ireland.

The fact that West Ham had only become a Parliamentary borough, with two divisions, in 1885, meant that there were no longstanding political traditions to be overcome. New ideas were easier to put over in a new and expanding community.

Chance, however, played a key role in Keir Hardie's success, as Caroline Benn and others have pointed out in their writings on this episode.* The leading Liberal contender for the seat, James Hume Webster, who had strong support within the constituency, shot himself six months before the election, leaving his supporters without an agreed alternative. The result was that Keir Hardie had a clear run and beat his Conservative opponent, George Banes. He gave support to the Liberal programme as far as it went, but reserved the right to support the interests of the workers irrespective of the exigencies of party welfare. W R Powell's narrative goes through this in admirable detail.

Although Keir Hardie lost the seat three years later, in 1895, and was criticised for the manner in which he had fulfilled his mandate, he had laid the foundations for Labour. Will Thorne, who succeeded him as the Labour candidate, won the seat in 1906 and the area has remained solidly Labour ever since. The 1892 result was a key first step on the road that led to Labour supplanting the Liberals as the alternative to Conservative rule and to a succession of Labour governments.

The present Labour leader, Tony Blair, and his guru, Philip Gould, have suggested that in breaking with Liberalism Labour cut itself off from the other great radical force in British politics, thus weakening the alternative to Conservative rule - a view that few Labour stalwarts would accept. What happened in West Ham, as explained in W R Powell's study, was an important part of this development which was, from any point of view, crucial for the history of politics in twentieth century Britain.

Stan Newens

*See Caroline Benn, *Keir Hardie*, Hutchinson, London, 1992, p. 85.

4

Keir Hardie in West Ham: "A constituency with a past."[1]

In July 1892 the parliamentary division of West Ham South elected James Keir Hardie as one of the first independent Labour MPs in the country. He lost the seat three years later, and never regained it. These events have often been discussed in the context of Hardie's career and the origins of the Labour movement.[2] The present paper explores the local background of the episode, from 1880 to 1895.

In 1895, a few months after Hardie had been defeated, John Spencer Curwen, who had been one of his supporters, gave a lecture on the recent election, entitled "A constituency with a past".[3] He meant a dubious past, in the sense used by Oscar Wilde in *Lady Windermere's Fan* ("...many a woman has a past, but ... she has at least a dozen.")

By the 1880s West Ham, adjoining London to the east of the river Lea, was a booming industrial town, with a population approaching 200,000. It became a municipal borough in 1886 and a county borough in 1889. From 1880, as part of the South Essex (Romford) parliamentary division, it was represented by two Conservatives, the banker Thomas Baring, and William Makins, chairman of the Great Eastern Railway, whose carriage works were at Stratford in West Ham. The prospective Liberal candidates were Edward North Buxton, a Whig brewer, and Edward Rider Cook, a radical soap manufacturer at Stratford.[4] By then both the Liberals and the Conservatives had associations in South Essex, with branches in West Ham. The Liberals were the more active. Between 1880 and 1886 they held 130 meetings in West Ham, including many small, educational lectures. The Conservatives held only 19, usually large rallies, like the one in May 1882 attended by Lord Salisbury, the future prime minister.[5]

Under the Franchise Act (1884), and the Redistribution Act (1885) West Ham became a parliamentary borough with two divisions, North and South, each with one member. Both divisions were fiercely contested in the following years.[6] In 1885 the Conservative leader was Major George Banes of Plaistow, partner in a firm of wharfingers.[7] Bald and thickset, with Dundreary whiskers, he posed as a plain man, unambitious, devoted to the public good, and a friend of the workers, while advocating peace, retrenchment, reform, and defence of the Empire.[8] He was actually tough and shrewd, with long experience on the West Ham local board, the school board, and a volunteer artillery company, which he himself had raised. He was courteous, friendly and laconic, though capable of forceful speech. Among other prominent Conservatives were David Howard, chemical manufacturer, and Philip Savill, brewer, both at Stratford.[9]

The Liberals were led by Frederick C Blackburn, who had been trained in Birmingham by Francis Schnadhorst, and in 1877 was appointed agent and secretary of the West Ham Liberal Association.[10] Most of them were radicals, advocating universal (male) suffrage; one man, one vote; the payment of MPs; land reform; free primary education; the reform or abolition of the House of Lords; Irish Home Rule; and a peaceful foreign policy.[11] Among the radicals, uneasily yoked, were two groups, nonconformists and seculars. The nonconformists' leaders were J Spencer Curwen, musicologist, local historian, and member of Stratford Congregational Church,[12] and Dr John Moir, medical practitioner at Canning Town and a member of West Ham school board, who was also a vice-president of the Scottish Labour Party.[13] Besides the main radical programme, these nonconformists favoured the disestablishment of the Church of England and temperance reform.

The secular radicals, who were in varying degrees hostile to the churches, were locally active and aggressive. In 1881 they opened the "Cromwell Patriotic Club and Institute" near Plaistow railway station.[14] During the following years, under the leadership of William Volckman, a Stratford jam manufacturer, and Edward Fulcher, a builder, the club mounted an extensive programme of lectures, concerts, and social events for working men. Several meetings were held in support of Charles Bradlaugh's refusal to swear an oath on the Bible when admitted as an MP.[15] Bradlaugh himself addressed the club at least twice.[16] Another well-known speaker was the theosophist Annie Besant.[17] In 1883 three lectures on "The Origin of Man" were given by Edward Aveling, then a prominent radical and later a socialist agitator.[18] He condemned the Bible as scientifically worthless, and gave a Darwinian view: "Man was constantly evolving, and there was bright hope for the future ... the world would go on upward, higher and higher, and greater happiness to all would be the result."[19] He is said to have been a brilliant speaker. But his high-flown sentiments at the Cromwell Club read ironically in view of his private life.[20] In the following year the militant atheist G W Foote, an associate of Aveling, lectured to the club on his own recent imprisonment for blasphemy, under the title "How I fell among thieves".[21]

The club had a concert hall for 500, bar, billiard room, library, and roof-garden.[22] Its programmes included "humorous readings" by the secretary, J S Chapman,[23] "a farce and scenes from Shakespeare",[24] and later a dinner and concert, sponsored by the West Ham branch of the National Secular Society.[25]

In 1884 the club held several meetings in support of parliamentary reform.[26] In 1885, with a general election approaching, it promoted the nomination of William Volckman as the Liberal candidate for West Ham South. The Liberals had agreed that their candidates for both borough constituencies should be chosen by an elected caucus of 500 members: 250 for West Ham North, and 250 for the South. The caucus system, developed in Birmingham, was designed to make the selection of candidates more democratic, and less susceptible to influence and money.[27] It was hated and feared by the Conservatives,[28] and disliked by some Liberals.[29] The members of each caucus were elected by a show of hands in a series of meetings in the constituency. How this was done at Plaistow, in West Ham South, on 2 February 1885, was described by a witness writing as "Liberty-loving Englishman".[30] At a meeting attended by some 80 men, mostly Cromwell club members:

> As the chairman read out the name of the candidate, a dark-whiskered gentleman in the corner of the room, if he was in favour of the candidate, shouted "up", and the hands went up. But if the candidate did not meet with his approval he was silent, and no one voted. And these men, who are elected in this manner, set themselves up as representing the electors of West Ham.

This account drew a comment from Spencer Curwen.[31] He agreed that the description of the Plaistow meeting was accurate: the Workmen's [i.e. Cromwell] Club had formed about four-fifths of those attending, and had the elections entirely in their hands. But, he added, who is to blame? Those who didn't come, including several ministers. Curwen hoped that next year the election of Plaistow's 91 caucus members would be more widely representative. This letter shows the gulf between the nonconformist and the secular radicals, and particularly the nonconformists' dislike of the Cromwell Club.

William Volckman's bandwagon as the prospective Liberal candidate gathered speed, and on 10 April he topped the poll in a nomination ballot held at Stratford, defeating Joseph Leicester, a trade unionist and temperance reformer.[32] This vote was challenged as irregular by W H Smith and others, who said that they would oppose Volckman because he had failed to defend the labour interests of the constituency, because he was the nominee of Bradlaugh and the Cromwell Club, and because he had slandered Joseph Leicester. Volckman, he added, was not acceptable to the "Temperance 250", which was strongly represented in the caucus, nor to religious people.[33] This diatribe was effectively refuted by the West Ham Liberal Club, the Cromwell Club, and Volckman himself, who said that the proposal to invite him to stand had come from two deputations comprising electors from every polling district, and at least six associations.[34] On 22 May Volckman's candidature was approved "by a considerable majority" at another caucus meeting, at Plaistow.[35]

On 30 May 1885 Frederick Blackburn stated in the press that according to his records, Volckman had "honourably submitted" to every vote that had been taken and that he had topped the poll on four occasions.[36] The last vote had been "simply one of etiquette, as between the north and south divisions" [of West Ham], to confirm the selection already made by the southern division, "who on this occasion attended in far greater force than those of the northern, many of which ... abstained from voting ... while a large proportion voted with the minority." Blackburn added that in due course there would be another meeting of the electors to confirm the choice of candidate. William Volckman had no reason to fear this test, and hoped that it would put an end to bickering.

It seems from Blackburn's letter and other newspaper reports that the choice of the Liberal candidate for West Ham South, made initially by the caucus of 250 electors for that constituency, was thought to need confirmation by the full caucus of 500 for the whole borough. A meeting of the full caucus had already approved Volckman's selection, but since it had been poorly attended by northern electors, there was to be a final meeting for the same purpose.

Blackburn evidently favoured Volckman, but his influence was abruptly removed when he collapsed and died on 31 May, only twenty four hours after the publication of the letter.[37] On 9 June, at the final confirmation meeting, Volckman's candidature was defeated by 248 votes to 245.[38] In the preceding debate he had defended his association with Bradlaugh, while denying that he himself was himself an atheist. Spencer Curwen said that he opposed Volckman not because of his principles, his public capacity, nor his religious opinions, but because he could not win parliamentary election owing to "other matters to which it was quite impossible he could refer at that meeting". The "other matters" may have concerned Volckman's wife Elizabeth, a French woman usually known as "Madame Volckman". On two occasions, in later years, she took action for slander. The first was in 1891, when it had been alleged that she and William were not married.[39] In the following year she won damages against two former friends who had said that she had murdered her first husband and had been hounded out of Paris by the police for keeping a brothel.[40] Such rumours, however false, would have told against her husband as parliamentary candidate, but the main objections to his candidature were probably his position as a wealthy factory owner, and his connection with the Cromwell Club.[41]

Almost immediately after the adverse vote of 9 June William Volckman resigned his candidature.[42] On 22 June W H Smith chaired a meeting in Canning Town which resolved to back Joseph Leicester as the "Labour and Radical" candidate.[43] On the 27th a deputation of 50 from "the Liberal and Radical societies of South West Ham" waited on Volckman at his home in the wealthy residential area of Knotts Green, Leyton, to urge him to reconsider his retirement.[44] In a high-minded reply Volckman said that he would do so only as the candidate of a united party. He had retired because the caucus had become a battleground of contending clubs whose main aim was not the choice of candidate, but a monopoly of the act of choosing. He agreed that it would be desirable to chose a Labour candidate for West Ham South but why go to Lambeth to find one [Joseph Leicester]? He again denied that he had tried to foist himself on the constituency, and condemned Leicester for encouraging violence against opponents. He hoped that the West Ham caucus would be split into two distinct bodies, for the North and South divisions, each responsible for electing its own candidate. The caucus for West Ham South might then be increased by 50, to allow for its larger population.

In the following months Joseph Leicester was gradually accepted as the Liberal candidate for West Ham South. Among his supporters was Henry Worland, a Canning Town corn merchant who was for many years prominent in the public life of West Ham: "a strong, strenuous, man ... firmer, graver, more prudent every year".[45]

Leicester's success may have owed something to the closure of the Cromwell Club. In August 1885 it was reported that the club was being prosecuted for selling liquor to non-members.[46] It still survived in September, when it was said to be threatening action against supporters of Joseph Leicester, but by 17 October the club premises had been sold to the new vicar of Plaistow, Thomas Given-Wilson, who in December reopened it as a church mission hall and club.[47] Given-Wilson later mentioned the Cromwell club in a published description of Plaistow as it had been when he arrived in 1884:[48]

> ... A great population, some given over to dissent, but more sunk into actual heathenism, among whom the Atheists were making triumphant progress, hundreds crowding to the notorious Cromwell club to hear Bradlaugh, Mrs Besant and the like rave out blasphemous infidelity, robbing the poor creatures who listened open-mouthed, of the only thing that could make their sad, suffering, diseased existences endurable: the hope of immortality, the faith in a loving and merciful Father, and in a Saviour who was afflicted in all their afflictions.

This effusion was part of the tendentious scheme by which Given-Wilson attracted donations towards philanthropic work in Plaistow by proclaiming the miseries of his parishioners.[49] But it scarcely exaggerated the loathing provoked in some hearts by the Cromwell Club.

On 26 September 1885 it was announced that the West Ham Radical Alliance Club and Institute would soon be opening in temporary premises adjoining William Volckman's factory in High Street, Stratford.[50] It would promote radicalism through a club department (subscription 6 shillings a year) and a political department (1s. a year). There were said to be over 300 promises of membership. The club had been opened by 7 November, when it was stated also that Volckman was president of the newly-founded Radical Alliance.[51] This Stratford club was presumably intended to replace the Cromwell Club, but it is not known to have been involved in the politics of West Ham South. William Volckman himself finally threw his weight behind Joseph Leicester, and on 28 November, general election day, urged his friends to do the same.[52]

By 1885 dissatisfaction with the inadequate social policies of the Liberal leadership, and that of the secularists, was causing some radicals to gravitate to the Social Democratic Federation or the Socialist League. Others formed small, independent clubs which are hard to trace, probably because they avoided the kind of local publicity which might have endangered their members' jobs, at a time when socialists were generally regarded as dangerous revolutionaries. The history of one such club, skilfully pieced together by Mr S A Shipley, sheds light on West Ham's politics as well as the wider issues and activities of London socialism.[53]

The Stratford Dialectical and Radical Club (SDRC), meeting in the "Telegraph" public house in Leyton Road, was formed in November 1880 by seceding members of the local branch of the National Secular Society, led by "Captain" Tom Lemon, a former merchant seaman, now a Stratford pawnbroker, and Ambrose G Barker, a young schoolmaster. Both men had studied under Edward Aveling at the NSS's "Hall of Science". Lemon, who became president of the new club, in 1882 took over the "Telegraph" in succession to his uncle. Barker, secretary of the club, was the son of a Chartist. He had come up from Northamptonshire in 1878, to teach at the new board school in Church Road, Leyton.[54]

The club's meetings were advertised in the *National Reformer* and *Radical* magazines, and by handbills. They included educational as well as political lectures and classes, some given by Lemon and Barker, others by visiting speakers like those from the Social and Political Education League.[55] The club supported H M Hyndman's newly-formed Social Democratic Federation, to which both Lemon and Barker belonged. Barker became chairman of the *Freiheit* Defence Committee which opposed the prosecution of the German revolutionary Johann Most.[56] In April 1882 he represented the club at a meeting in London to welcome Russian revolutionaries, and in June invited one of them, Prince Pëtr Kropotkin, to lecture to the club.[57]

The SDRC seems to have had no links with the orthodox radical clubs of West Ham, or even with the Cromwell Club, but it did have dealings with a man who was deeply involved in local politics. This was Thomas M Kelly, who in September lectured to the club on "British commerce and labour in relation to foreign competition". He was then described as secretary of the Anti-Sugar Bounty League.[58] The sugar refineries at Silvertown, in South West Ham, were then losing trade to foreign competitors receiving state bounties.[59] Since they employed 500 workers, nearly all men, sugar bounties were a major issue in local politics.[60] Thomas Kelly's lecture evidently went down well, for he was invited back the following week. But he was not what he may have seemed to be. He and his friend Samuel Peters were the leaders of a gang using bogus trade unions to promote the interests of employers and the Conservative party by strike-breaking and other methods.[61] Their activities in West Ham South during the general elections of 1885 and 1886 are mentioned below.

In August 1884 the SDRC took part in the great demonstration at Wanstead in aid of parliamentary reform.[62] Speeches on that occasion were made from four platforms, one of which was chaired by Tom Lemon. This is the last known reference to the club. Its secretary, Ambrose Barker, remained an assistant teacher in the same school for 44 years.[63] Intelligent and cultured, he collected rare books,

10

and wrote several books himself. He was always eager to join revolutionary associations, and for ten years edited the anarchist journal *Freedom*.

The president of the SDRC, Tom Lemon, has been traced no later than 1887.[64] He was an ambivalent and somewhat sinister figure. Having founded and led this radical club, he later worked for the Conservatives in the general elections of 1885 and 1886. His early life seems to have been colourful and mysterious, and was said to have included service in the American Civil War.[65] He was a freemason, a financial speculator, and a collector of jade and Edison-Bell gramophone records. Mr Shipley calls him "a dyed in the wool Tory democrat". If this implies fixed political principles, it was not the view of some who observed his actions in 1885-87.[66]

On 15 January 1885 a public meeting was held at Tidal Basin to promote Lt-Col P Cowan, alderman and a former sheriff of London, as the "accepted industrial candidate" for West Ham South.[67] Several leading Conservatives attended, including their agent for South Essex, R T Wragg. The meeting was chaired by Tom Lemon, who was said to represent "the Seamen's Society and other radical associations", and to be president of the "industrial committee". The other members of that committee were named as Samuel Peters (Sugar Operatives Society), vice-president; John McLean (cooper) and Thomas Kelly (Dock Labourers' Society), joint honorary secretaries. These particulars, with the report on the meeting, indicate that Lemon was now closely associated with the Kelly-Peters gang. In presenting Cowan, Lemon said that when sheriff, he had urged that the labour interest should be represented in the London Chamber of Commerce, but that the "monied mob of the Chamber" would not listen. Cowan himself stressed the need to protect British trade, especially from foreign sugar bounties.[68]

The meeting went badly for the organizers. One heckler shouted "Has Mr Lemon gone from Radical to Conservative?". When asked who invited him to be a candidate, Cowan replied vaguely that it was the Conservative Club of West Ham, "men whom I understood to be the Industrial Three Hundred in this district". Under further questioning Lemon was forced to admit that he had invited Cowan "on my own individual responsibility". Asked what connection he had with the constituency, Lemon said that he had had a vote in South Essex and would probably have one in West Ham South. In view of his long-standing connection with West Ham North this was a disingenuous reply, though not necessarily false in those days of multiple voting. Lemon then added that he had an interest in the constituency "as one, if not of the working class, then of the class which immediately overlies the working class". "You are a paid agent!" shouted a heckler. A resolution adopting Cowan was moved by John McLean, and was declared by Lemon to be carried, but an amendment rejecting him, moved by James Ronan, vice-president of the Canning Town, Plaistow, and Silvertown Radical Association, was overwhelmingly carried. In the following month, Cowan, "not finding a very cordial reception" in West Ham, announced that he had become the Conservative candidate for Tower Hamlets, Whitechapel.[69]

In July 1885 the Conservatives adopted William Pearce, of J Elder & Co., shipowners, as their candidate for West Ham South.[70] When he fell ill and withdrew, they accepted an offer to succeed him by Alfred Pound of Wroxall (Isle of Wight), a former colonial magistrate from Eton and Oxford.[71] Though unwelcome to those who wanted a working man to represent them, he won over the sugar workers by promising to oppose foreign bounties, and also gained the support of Major Banes.[72] But at the general election on 5 December 1885 Joseph Leicester, standing as a "Labour" candidate with Liberal support, defeated Pound by 3527 votes to 2545. The Liberals also won West Ham North, though by a smaller majority.[73]

At the 1886 general election Joseph Leicester again contested West Ham South. In the Liberal split over Irish Home Rule he remained loyal to Gladstone. That must have cost him some Liberal Unionist votes, while the Irish vote, which might have helped him, was not yet properly organized.[74] During the election campaign he was damaged by some slanderous attacks from the Kelly-Peters gang, failed to convince some former supporters that he had been a good MP, and made one or two silly speeches.[75] And he found himself opposed by a strong local candidate.

In April 1886 George Banes was nominated as Conservative candidate for West Ham South, at a meeting said to have included "several prominent Liberals".[76] Early in May, at a Primrose League meeting in Plaistow, he said that he had been brought up as a Liberal and was still one essentially, since his Conservatism "embraced the old Liberal principles of hatred of tyranny, of kindness and help to their fellow men."[77] That was not entirely humbug, for only a few months earlier Spencer Curwen had publicly commended Banes for his interest in progress.[78] In June Banes was challenged by Edwin Newman, who came forward as an "Independent and Progressive Conservative", advocating "the rights of British labour".[79] Newman was one of the Kelly-Peters gang.[80] At an adoption meeting late in June his candidature was proposed by Kelly and supported by Tom Lemon.[81] But a week later, with their approval, Newman announced that he was withdrawing to avoid splitting the Conservative vote.[82] It seems more than likely that Newman's candidature was from the first a tactical move designed to assist Banes. Whether Banes connived at it is another matter. But in any case Kelly and Peters would have hoped to gain credit from his election, which duly took place on 7 July 1886, when he defeated Leicester by 2778 votes to 2472. At the same time the Conservatives gained West Ham North, unseating the Gladstonian Liberal MP.[83]

The Conservative government of Lord Salisbury, lasting from 1886 to 1892, was one of the longest in the 19th century. George Banes, MP throughout those years, was once criticised for his silence in Parliament by Spencer Curwen, who likened him to the sailor's parrot: "Can he talk? No, but see how wise he looks."[84] Banes himself complained in 1892 that there had been scarcely any chance for a Conservative member to speak in Parliament unless he was connected with the ministry.[85] In local affairs, during those years, he remained quietly active, with a relaxed attitude to party politics. He remarked in 1889:

> I honestly try to do the best I can, without making a great fuss over it, for the interests of my constituents ... I am perfectly free, and no party or personal considerations will ever induce me to vote or act against my conscientious convictions.[86]

This lofty attitude may have inhibited Conservative activity in the constituency at a time when the Liberals, in spite of internal divisions, were full of fight and constantly in the public eye. During the great dock strike of 1889, for example, when Banes claimed to be working for a settlement, he was upstaged by Hume Webster and his Liberals, who got much credit for supporting the strikers.[87]

After his election defeat Joseph Leicester was discarded as prospective candidate for West Ham South. A writer with the pen-name "A Liberal who wants to win", described him as "a very good man, but as a politician a great failure ... a windbag", and this seems to have been the general view.[88] Leicester had also suffered from financial difficulties arising from his position as a "Labour" MP, dependent on local subscriptions to meet his election expenses.[89] A candidate who was wealthy as well as radical would be attractive, and such a man now appeared.

James Hume Webster, born in 1843 at Montrose (Forfar), was the son of a customs officer, and a great-nephew of Joseph Hume MP (1777 - 1855), who had for thirty years led the radicals in parliament.[90] From modest beginnings he had prospered as a banker, and since 1879 he had been head of Hume Webster, Hoare & Co. in the City of London. He had a country seat at Marden Park, in Godstone (Surrey) and bred racehorses. In 1886 he had contested the South Essex (Romford) parliamentary division as a Gladstonian and had done well to come second to the winning Conservative, pushing the previous MP, now a Liberal Unionist, into third place.[91] After the 1886 election he had approached Hugh Reeves, Blackburn's successor as Liberal agent, with a view to standing for West Ham South. Reeves advised him to "go for it".[92]

Early in January 1887 Webster took part in a meeting in Canning Town convened to launch a "West Ham Central Liberal and Radical Association".[93] The platform speakers included W H Smith and Henry Worland (now an alderman), both former supporters of Leicester. They were constantly interrupted by protests - possibly justified - that the meeting was "a fraud ... a dodge to get the voters ... to recognise a 'split off' association as the head of the radical cause",[94] and that it had been got up in order to foist Hume Webster on the constituency. Later in January it was stated that there were eleven associations claiming to represent the different elements of Liberalism in West Ham South, and that one of them had approached Hume Webster.[95] Accompanying that report was an account of another meeting in Canning Town to promote Webster's candidature. It was attended by Henry Labouchere, the maverick MP for Northampton, who spoke in Webster's favour. Like the previous meeting it provoked fierce opposition, which by a large majority passed a motion demanding a wider choice, and preferably a Labour candidate.

In spite of these setbacks, Hume Webster persisted with his candidature. His local supporters, besides W H Smith and Worland, included William Volckman, Richard High, and Edward Fulcher, now a borough councillor, all former members of the Cromwell Club.[96] Webster also had influential friends among radicals outside West Ham, including five MPs: Henry Labouchere, Sir Wilfrid Lawson, Charles A V Conybeare, Thomas P O'Connor, and Joseph Arch.[97] Labouchere gave Webster much support in the constituency during the following years, while O'Connor and Lawson occasionally came down for meetings.

Hume Webster was a firm but moderate radical, and does not seem to have been personally unlikeable. But many radicals resented him as a rich carpet-bagger imposed upon them by Volckman and extremists like Labouchere. Nonconformists disapproved of Webster's racehorses, while temperance reformers doubted his commitment to their cause. Webster's opponents, led by Dr John Moir, brought forward as their candidate William Morgan, a London businessman who was said to be a trade unionist, and to have worked at one time for a weekly wage; but he withdrew in July.[98] John Spencer Curwen was then persuaded to oppose Webster, in the absence of a Labour man "of their wage-earning class". He opened his campaign in September 1887.[99]

Hume Webster and Spencer Curwen confronted each for over two years. The local caucus system had now broken down, and occasional attempts to restore Liberal unity in the constituency came to nothing. The rivals were unevenly matched. Curwen, long established in West Ham, was a high-minded intellectual with a small local business. While devoted to reform on Christian principles, and to temperance, he was not personally ambitious, and shrank from front-line politics. One of his principal supporters, saying that there was "no go" in him, went over to Webster.[100] Another critic, though admitting that Curwen was a good radical, pointed out that he was deaf: "how, therefore, can he be of use in the House of Commons?"[101]

Webster was a forceful self-made man of wide experience. He had evidently enjoyed his baptism of political fire in South Essex, and relished the thought of another such battle. The challenge of West Ham South was, perhaps, its main attraction, since he could almost certainly have found a safe seat elsewhere. His views on the question of a working-class MP were sensible if not sensitive. Such a man, he told one audience, would have to be paid. He went on:

There is nothing very technical in a working man's life in West Ham, and after all, is there not more advantage in a knowledge of the world, of the men in Parliament and of the permanent government officials that he has to meet in connexion with his work? My experience in life has given me the possession of that knowledge, and the fact that I know three quarters of the present House of Commons is to your advantage ... because no one, however good or able, could stand or do much alone. [102]

Webster pursued his candidature with energy and skill, paying particular attention to canvassing, and issuing frequent lists of a "general committee" of men pledged to vote for him at the next election. He claimed 1,400 such adherents in May 1887, 2,000 in May 1888, 3,130 in October 1888.[103] At the same time he supported many Liberals appealing for registration at the electoral revision courts. In December 1890 he claimed that since 1887 he had been successful in 1,087 appeals, compared with a combined total of 363 by other Liberal agents and the Conservatives.[104] In the same period he held 113 public meetings, as against 63 by the Curwenites and 17 by the Conservatives.[105]

A progressive feature of Webster's campaign was the formation of a Women's Liberal Association, with Mrs Labouchere as president.[106] He also gave generously to good causes, providing entertainment as well as political rhetoric. In January 1889, for example, he chaired a concert at Canning Town in aid of the Holy Trinity church schools.[107] The programme included a toy band, conducted by Mrs Hume Webster, and featuring a triangle, a quail-pipe, drums, cuckoo (Miss Hume Webster), trumpets, nightingale (Hume Beckles), jingles, violin (Master Noel Hume Webster), whistles, and piano. Miss Hume Webster sang and recited, and Alderman Worland sang comic songs such as "Call her back and kiss her" and "The doctor says I'm not to be worried". In April 1888 Webster gave a free tea for 500 poor children of Tidal Basin.[108] In the following August he entertained 700 children from West Ham, Leyton and Walthamstow at Marden Park, where they admired his German wolfhound, Marco, a beast bred in Central Africa and measuring 6 feet 6 inches from nose to tail.[109]

Webster's opponents particularly resented his frequent references to the financial contributions that he was prepared to make as a candidate. These implied, said Curwen, that "he will crush with his gold any man who lives to oppose him".[110] But Webster was unrepentant, saying that his political expenditure was within normal limits, while he did not make charitable gifts unless asked to do so.[111] There is no doubt that his generosity strengthened his position. So, also, did his readiness to identify himself with working men by joining friendly societies and trade unions.[112] And he devoted much time as well as money to the constituency. In December 1890 he said that in the past four years he had spent on average two or three nights a week there.[113]

Most notable of all Hume Webster's activities in West Ham was his support of the dockers during their celebrated "tanner a day" strike in 1889.[114] There was much local sympathy for the strikers, and when those in West Ham's docks came out late in August, Alderman Henry Phillips pressed for a settlement and launched a relief fund. Hume Webster promptly offered to subscribe £25 a day to the fund for the duration of the strike. He was later said to have subscribed that amount for seven days, as well as smaller sums, while his radical club in Barking Road, Canning Town, provided many free meals for strikers. He also joined in the negotiations which in mid-September settled the strike in the dockers' favour. While his help may not have been crucial to their success, it had been substantial, and earned him great credit. Early in the strike Phillips told the dockers that Webster had been the first [outsider?] to come to them in their hour of need, and that they would not forget him; and at a victory rally after the strike Webster's arrival was greeted with three cheers.

Webster was not unduly disturbed by general criticisms of his wealth, arrogance, and lack of initial support. But when it was suggested or implied that he was guilty of malpractice he immediately threatened legal action. This happened at least twice. On the first occasion Curwen was forced to deny that he had any intention of accusing Webster of corruption.[115] Webster accepted this assurance. But a few months later he brought a slander action against (Sir) William Randal Cremer, MP for Shoreditch, Haggerston, for remarks made at one of Curwen's meetings.[116] This case seems to have arisen from an infelicitous reference by Webster to "a bastard working man". He meant a working man who had risen to become a capitalist, but his opponents seized upon it as a rod to beat him with.[117] Eventually Cremer also apologised for his remarks.[118]

Curwen and his friends deserve credit for their determined opposition to such a powerful adversary. That they shrank from confronting Webster in the law courts is not surprising. Meanwhile, however, he continued to gain support. In 1887 three borough council members can be identified as his adherents as against 10 Curwenites and 9 Conservatives. By 1890 he had 13 supporters on the council, more than Curwen (5) and the Conservatives (5) combined.[119] At the council elections in 1889 five Websterites, out of six vacancies, headed the polls in Canning Town and Plaistow wards.[120] Webster had fewer nonconformist ministers behind him than did Curwen, but more Irish voters, Roman Catholic priests, and trade unionists.

In November 1889 Arnold Morley, Liberal chief whip in the House of Commons, suggested the appointment of an arbitrator to decide between Webster and Curwen, one of whom would then retire, enabling the local party to unite behind the survivor.[121] Negotiations commenced, but on 3 December a mass meeting of Webster's supporters voted against arbitration. He himself was ill and could not attend, but his secretary, J Ledger Keating, speaking for him, emphasised Webster's support for the dockers, the triumph of his supporters in the council elections, and the accession to his cause of Alderman Phillips and other local leaders. The meeting reached its decision because they felt that Webster was now strong enough to win even a three-cornered election, and because they had heard that three of Curwen's main supporters would not accept any arbitration favouring Webster and might promote another candidate if Curwen withdrew. A month later Curwen did indeed withdraw, mounting a bitter attack on Webster and saying that he himself was making way for a candidate who would command irresistible support.[122] In accepting his resignation his committee thought that a coalition would now take place between the Curwenites and "a considerable party who have hitherto held aloof from both candidates".

Webster's recent illness had been due to ulcers on his vocal chords. It was said to be dangerous, and he was treated by Sir Morell Mackenzie, a specialist on throat cancer.[123] But he recovered, and at the end of January was able to attend a meeting in Canning Town addressed by T P O'Connor, who had come at Arnold Morley's request to urge the local Liberals to unite behind Webster.[124] For a few weeks Webster seemed to possess the field, but his opponents were implacable, and brought forward a formidable new candidate.

James Keir Hardie (1856 - 1915), like Hume Webster, was a Scotsman.[125] Born in Lanarkshire, he had become a miner, a trade union leader and a journalist. In 1888 he had contested Mid-Lanarkshire as an Independent Labour candidate in a parliamentary by-election. In the same year he became secretary of the newly-founded Scottish Labour Party, whose president was Robert B Cunninghame Graham, MP for NW Lanarkshire, and vice-president Dr John Moir.[126] Graham, Moir, and W Randal Cremer are all credited with inviting Keir Hardie to West Ham.[127]

Keir Hardie had no previous connection with West Ham or with Essex. He proceeded cautiously, seeking selection on his own merits, and not as the creature of the Curwenite diehards, while aiming to win over the nonconformists and temperance reformers. At a meeting on 16 April 1890 he confined himself to a general lecture on "Labour politics", and obtained a resolution favouring the election of "a *bona fide* representative of working class interests, who in addition to being a Home Rule Liberal, will also strive to secure for labour a better share of the comforts and enjoyments of life".[128] At another meeting, a week later, his supporters included Cunninghame Graham and Josiah Foster, minister of the Victoria Docks Baptist Church.[129] It was then reported that twelve nonconformist ministers had recently pledged their support for Hardie's views. The meeting passed a resolution in favour of a labour representative for West Ham South, but the chairman, Councillor William East, disallowed a motion naming Keir Hardie as the candidate. Hardie himself added that "the wooing was going on nicely; they did not want to hurry matters or frighten the people they were trying to woo, and he thought it would be out of place if they made any announcement that night".

On 17 May an open-air meeting of some 250 working men in Canning Town, with few dissentients, adopted Keir Hardie as their candidate "in the Labour and Home Rule interest".[130] For the next twenty months Hardie maintained his candidature in the face of fierce attack from the Websterites. He was a charismatic speaker, dedicated to the Labour movement; and he soon gained the backing of Will Thorne, a rising young trade union leader, who in 1891 was elected to the borough council.[131] But Webster's greater resources enabled him, as before, to undertake more activities than his rival, and thus to gain more publicity. He held 24 meetings to Hardie's 10 in 1890, and 23 to 12 in 1891. His supporters on the borough council numbered 13 to Hardie's 5 in 1890, and 13 to 8 in 1891.

Webster's work in the registration courts was also going well, and early in 1891 brought him the adherence of John Walsh, a leading radical who had been one of his critics.[132] By then Webster was claiming 3,600 "committee" members, and that 600 more were expected after the publication of the next electoral register.[133] In July 1891 Keir Hardie alleged that Webster had offered him £150 to withdraw from the constituency.[134] Webster denied it. It seems likely that Hardie had been offered repayment of his out-of-pocket expenses if he retired, but whether the initial approach came from him, from Webster, or from one of their agents without the prior knowledge of the principals, remains doubtful. In any case the negotiations came to nothing.

In December 1891 Webster's "committee" was said to have reached 4,496, with 526 more expected next year.[135] On the 5th he attended the third annual concert and dance of the South West Ham Women's Liberal Assocation.[136] In mid-January 1892 he joined with fellow countrymen, including his arch-opponent John Moir, in a Grand Scottish gathering in Silvertown.[137] But on 29 January he was found dead in the grounds of his estate at Marden Park.[138]

Hume Webster had been shot through the mouth, and there was a revolver in his hand. He had been suffering from the current epidemic of "Russian flu" and had complained of his throat. It was suggested that he had been fearing the recurrence of the ulcers from which he had suffered in 1889. An inquest decided that he had committed suicide while temporarily insane.[139] A fact not mentioned in the published report on the inquest was the illness of Sir Morell Mackenzie, who actually died only five days after Webster.[140] The loss of the doctor who had treated his throat in 1889 might well have intensified Webster's depression. A leading article on Webster's death commented that no one could look at him without being impressed by a sense of [resolution and tenacity] largely developed in him ... Nothing about him betokened yielding or weakness."[141] He was buried at Marden, "a kind, generous man, who will be missed by many a toiler and many a trade unionist".[142] He had been a central figure in one of the most notable episodes of West Ham's history, and was at the peak of his achievement when he died. Now he is now almost forgotten.[143]

Keir Hardie, though strengthened by Webster's death, was still opposed by some former Websterites, who cast around for a new candidate.[144] Hardie was uncompromising. He would not seek official recognition from the Liberal Party, nor would he negotiate with the Websterites.[145] On Sunday 27 March, at Mansfield House university settlement, Canning Town, he preached an afternoon sermon on the prophet Elijah and God's "still small voice" (I Kings, 19.11), and in the evening adopted a prophetic role himself, with a lecture urging the formation of an independent labour party.[146]

On 8 April a meeting of Websterites chaired by Alderman Henry Worland and including Councillors Edward Fulcher and Thomas Walsh, adopted Joseph Leicester, the former MP, as the "Radical and Labour" candidate for the constituency.[147] But Alderman Henry Phillips, who had been a leading adherent of Webster, refused to join them, adopting a neutral stance between the candidates.[148]

Leicester, who had been rejected six years earlier both by the electors and his constituency party, was not now a serious candidate. At the end of April, with a general election imminent, Keir Hardie's supporters stepped up their campaign.[149] On 18 June there was a trade union demonstration at Tidal Basin in which Hardie was pulled through the streets in a "monster boat" called *The Undaunted*.[150] He addressed six meetings on the 20th and others during the following days.[151] On 2 July it was announced that Joseph Leicester, after consulting Francis Schnadhorst, had withdrawn in Hardie's favour.[152] This is confirmed by a letter from Schnadhorst to Gladstone: "in South West Ham ... we acted just at the critical moment and have saved [the seat]".[153]

Keir Hardie's election address states that he has been invited unanimously by the "United Liberal, Radical and Labour Party of South West Ham" to stand as a "Labour, Radical and Home Rule candidate".[154] He agrees with the present programme of the Liberal Party so far as it goes, but reserves the right to take such action, irrespective of the exigencies of party welfare, as he thinks necessary in the interests of the workers. He favours separate parliaments for England, Scotland, and Wales as well as Ireland; the taxation of land values; the provision of houses for workers at low rents; the elimination of excessive working hours; public ownership of mines, banks, railways, docks and waterways; one man one vote; payment of MPs; disestablishment of the Church; pensions for all; and other measures (specified) in the workers' interests.

The Conservatives seem to have been inactive in the run-up to the general election, thinking that no effort was needed to ensure their victory. As one of them said in April, "instead of the Radicals fighting the Conservatives, they were more like Kilkenny cats, fighting against the Liberals".[155] He predicted that Banes would have the safest seat in the country.

When West Ham went to the polls on 4 July 1892 Keir Hardie defeated George Banes by 5,268 to 4,036.[156] The size of the majority - large for the time - must have been partly due to the national swing against the Conservatives. But it also reflected Hardie's personal appeal. A leader-writer thought that he "had got hold of the working men as no ordinary Liberal would have gripped them ... he is a man of ability, sincerity, and considerable force of character. His constituents believe in him thoroughly."[157] But Hardie certainly owed something to Hume Webster, particularly for his work in the registration courts. Hardie's election fund had totalled a modest £293, of which the *Workmen's Times* and the Scottish-born ironmaster Andrew Carnegie each subscribed £100. Later, during a strike at Carnegie's steelworks in Pittsburgh (Penn.), Hardie sent £100 to the strikers.[158]

During the next three years Keir Hardie's main concern was the distress caused by unemployment, and he laboured to persuade the government to look seriously at the problem.[159] On 14 December 1894 the Prime Minister, Lord Rosebery, came down to Stratford to give a public address. Before the meeting he received deputation from the West Ham Trades Council concerning unemployment. It was led by Hardie and Archibald Grove, the Liberal MP for West Ham North, who claimed that there were a million out of work in the country, and 5,000 in West Ham alone.[160] Rosebery cast doubt on these figures, and while admitting that unemployment was a great evil, said that, so far has he knew "no practical remedy has really been offered". He suggested that a formal petition, which Hardie had demanded, should be addressed to the Board of Trade. At the public meeting Rosebery made a brief, witty, but jejune speech urging Labour supporters to adhere to the Liberal Party, but containing no reference to unemployment.

Keir Hardie was furious at the Prime Minister's response to the deputation. At a meeting in Canning Town on 17 December he said that Rosebery had "come to them as if they were pantaloons at Christmas time, and had asked them to take part with him in his shameful and deliberate attempt to cheat the workers". He repeated the statement that there were a million unemployed, saying that it was based on Board of Trade figures, which were largely confined to skilled workers. He condemned the government for failing to introduce temperance legislation and payment of MPs, and thought that Liberals and Conservatives alike were mainly concerned "to obtain office and retain it as long as possible".

In January 1895 the West Ham Trades Council carried out a census of unemployment in the borough which proved that the situation was twice as bad as previously thought: 10,131 manual workers were unemployed including 9,500 males over 16, mainly married men; 7,969 of the total were in South West Ham.[161] White collar workers had not been counted. In February Hardie presented to the House of Commons a petition from the mayor and corporation of West Ham urging government action on unemployment. The House set up a select committee on the subject, at which he gave evidence.[162] Soon after that Rosebery's government fell. It would be more than ten years before a later Liberal government began to tackle unemployment. But Keir Hardie had been responsible for forcing the subject onto the political agenda, and in this his experience in West Ham played a valuable part.

Keir Hardie's criticism of the government in 1894-95 was not a new development. As an MP he was, from the first, determined to assert his independence, as he had frankly emphasised in the election address. He promptly demonstrated this by opposing the re-election of John Morley, the new Irish Secretary, as MP for Newcastle-upon-Tyne, because Morley was against statutory interference with the working hours of adult males.[163] This action angered some West Ham Liberals as well as the national leaders. Later in 1892, in a speech to the Congregational Union, Hardie denounced the churches for neglecting social problems: "The reason why the Labour party has turned its back on the church is because the church has turned its back on Christ in this matter. You preach to the respectability of your congregations ... you forget the withering and suffering masses outside the walls of your churches."[164] Hardie was howled down by the audience, though one minister admitted that his remarks, while exaggerated, contained much truth. The *Stratford Express* commented that the speech had upset some of Hardie's friends in West Ham, and that he must have forgotten how much he owed to the Congregational ministers in Plaistow and Canning Town.[165]

Keir Hardie's conduct in the House of Commons alienated many former supporters. His attendance record was poor, he denounced the two-party system, and by April 1894 was no longer taking the Liberal whip.[166] In June he caused outrage by his refusal to join in the motion congratulating the Queen on the birth of Prince Edward (Edward VIII), coupled with his cynically accurate prophesy concerning the prince's career.[167] He also offended the Irish over Home Rule, as described below. Alderman Worland, who had joined Hardie after Leicester's retirement, had already withdrawn his support.[168] Attempts were made in the autumn to promote a rival Liberal candidate for the constituency, but they came to nothing.[169]

In June 1895, with another general election imminent, the *Stratford Express* discussed the two candidates for West Ham South.[170] Banes was "the kind of man whom Englishmen delight to honour ... as near an approach to a typical John Bull as can be found - plain and straightforward ... heartily advocating everything likely to improve the condition of the people". But Keir Hardie was not viewed in the same light as three years ago. Then he had been regarded as:

> an extreme Radical with perhaps a little hankering after Socialism, whereas now he is referred to as a Socialist, who sometimes votes Radical in the House, and sometimes splits the Liberal vote, and so enables the Conservatives to win in working-class constituencies.

The writer added that Hardie's action in the House of Commons might cause many Liberals to go over to Banes; but he admitted that Hardie's action on unemployment during the previous winter had increased his popularity in the docks.

A few days before the election a mass meeting of Irishmen in Canning Town resolved not to support Keir Hardie at the polls, because he had broken his promise to put Home Rule first in his programme, and had opposed John Morley at Newcastle.[171] On the platform were several Roman Catholic priests. Among them was Timothy Ring from Silvertown, who shouted as the meeting closed: "Don't let hatred of the Tories stand between you and putting Keir Hardie out. We will vote for anyone to put him out."

When West Ham South went to the polls on 15 July 1895 George Banes regained the seat by 4,750 votes to Hardie's 3,975. In the following month Hardie, in a farewell speech in Canning Town before visiting the USA, said that he hoped to fight the constituency at the next election.[172] But in December Spencer Curwen brought a magisterial case against him in the lecture, mentioned at the beginning of this paper, on "A constituency with a past".[173] Displaying a chart of the polls in 1885, 1886, 1892 and 1895, he said that the progressives "had but to advance together and victory was secure. It was when the middle class sections held back that defeat came." Keir Hardie had offended the Irish and alarmed moderate voters by his advanced opinions. He had neglected his Parliamentary duties by attending only 174 divisions out of a possible 810 between 1892 and 1895. On the important Parish Councils Bill he had attended only 16 out of 113 divisions. Hardie had said that he hated Parliament, and that he was an agitator, not a statesman. But, said Curwen, an MP must be something of a statesman. He urged working men to take a more active interest in politics, while advising them, in order to win, to choose a "practical politician". Keir Hardie would no doubt find another constituency. He must never be brought forward in West Ham again. A new man would have a much better chance. In the discussion following the lecture some speakers were less critical of Hardie, but one of them thought that Labour's chances in West Ham had been "smashed for a generation" by Hardie's conduct.

Keir Hardie never again contested West Ham South. George Banes ("The sailor's parrot: can he talk? No, but see how wise he looks"), held the seat for the Conservatives until his retirement in 1906. But then, at last, the Labour Party won permanent control of it,[174] and Keir Hardie became an honoured name in West Ham, chosen by the borough council as the title of a great housing estate built after the Second World War.[175]

Sources

The main source of this paper is the *Stratford Express*. It was the leading local newspaper, founded in 1866, and owned by Wilson & Whitworth (*VCH Essex*, vi. 67, 87). The file in Newham reference library is virtually complete on microfilm for 1880 - 1895. Published weekly, it includes detailed, well-written and independent reports and comments on political events. Every issue during that period was examined for the present study, producing 840 (A4) pages of notes, to which were made a full personal name index and a selective subject index, to information on the West Ham South parliamentary constituency.

Acknowledgements

I am grateful to the Victoria County of Essex for six months study leave, during the 1970s, which made it possible to carry out the initial research for this paper, and to Stratford library, Newham, where the reference librarian, Mrs E Taylor, besides professional guidance, kindly ensured that I worked in comfort. The paper was put onto computer disk by Mrs. Helen Coghill, with assistance from Mrs. Pamela Studd, and my wife Avril has read the proofs. Their continuing help is much appreciated.

Author: W R Powell, 28 The Walnuts, Branksome Road, Norwich NR4 6SR.

Notes

1. This paper follows up work done by the writer for *VCH Essex* volume VI (1973). Most of the research for it was undertaken in the 1970s; and the detailed indexing in 1979 - 1980.

2. Good accounts can be found in P Thompson, *Socialists, Liberals and Labour: the Struggle for London, 1885-1914.* (1967); Kenneth Morgan, *Keir Hardie* (1975); F Reid, *Keir Hardie, the making of a Socialist* (1978).

3. *Stratford Express,* 7 December 1895.

4. E N Buxton (1840-1924), a noted philanthropist, was prominent in the preservation of Epping, Hainault, and Hatfield forests: *Essex Review,* xxxiii. 44 (obit.); *Who was Who.*

5. For the numbers of meetings, 1880-84, see *Stratford Express* reports. Lord Salisbury's visit: *Stratford Express,* 27 May 1882.

6. *VCH Essex,* vi. 112.

7. *Essex Leaders, Social and Political* (1906 edn.); *Essex Review,* xvi. 200 (obit.)

8. *Stratford Express,* 27 February, 25 July 1892; 6 July 1895.

9. For Howard: *Stratford Express,* 25 July, 26 September 1885; *VCH Essex,* vi. 78. For Savill: *Stratford Express,* 24 Dec 1887, 19 Dec 1891; *VCH Essex,* vi. 81. For Gray: *Stratford Express,* 3 July 1886; *VCH Essex,* vi. 88.

10. *Stratford Express,* 24 January, 7 and 14 February, 10 April 1880.

11. *Stratford Express,* 17 September 1887, speech by J Spencer Curwen.

12. *VCH Bibliography* (1959), 78; D McDougall, *Fifty years a borough ... the story of West Ham* (1936), 239.

13. F Reid, *op. cit.,* 128, 136. Many references in *Stratford Express,* including 13 June 1880 (School board); 28 March 1885 (temperance); 14 May 1892 (letter re W Ham politics).

14. *Stratford Express,* 26 March, 14 May, 24 September 1881.

15. *Stratford Express,* 14 May 1881; 27 January 1883; 23 January 1884.

16. *Stratford Express,* 8 April 1882; 27 January 1883.

17. *Stratford Express,* 14 June 1884. For Mrs Besant see: *DNB*; Y Kapp, *Eleanor Marx,* i. 268n.

18. *Stratford Express,* 30 June, 8 September, 13 October 1883.

19. *Stratford Express,* 30 June 1883.

20. Y Kapp, *op. cit.,* i. 261-272. Aveling was the lover of Karl Marx's daughter Eleanor, who was driven to suicide by his unkindness.

21. *Stratford Express,* 15 March 1884; Y Kapp, *op. cit.,* i. 269.

22. *Stratford Express,* 24 September 1881.

23. *Stratford Express,* 8 October 1881.

24. *Stratford Express,* 30 September 1882.

25. *Stratford Express,* 12 January 1884.

26. *Stratford Express,* 3 May, 6 July, 27 August, 13 Dec 1884.

27. *Stratford Express,* 24 January 1885, speech by Andrew Johnston.

28. *Stratford Express,* 27 May 1882 (T C Baring); 23 February 1884 (George Banes).

29. E.g. Matthew Gray, of the Silvertown Rubber Co: *Stratford Express,* 24 January 1885.

30. *Stratford Express,* 7 February 1885.

31. *Stratford Express,* 14 February 1885.

32. *Stratford Express,* 7, 21 March, 11 April 1885.

33. *Stratford Express,* 18 April 1885. The "Temperance 250" was a pressure group organized on lines similar to those of the Liberal caucus. Dr John Moir was among its leaders: *Stratford Express,* 11 April 1885, p. 5.

34. *Stratford Express,* 18 April 1885.

35. *Stratford Express,* 23 May 1885.

36. *Stratford Express,* 30 May 1885. The minutes kept by Blackburn are not known to have survived.

37. *Stratford Express,* 6 June 1885.

38. *Stratford Express,* 13 June 1885.

39. *Stratford Express,* 25 April 1891.

40. *Stratford Express,* 16 January 1892.

41. One of his supporters said that the "two minorities" who had worked against Volckman at the caucus were the "socialistic Radicals" and "the Whigs": *Stratford Express,* 4 July 1885.

42. On 13 July, according to his later statement: *Stratford Express,* 8 August 1885.

43. *Stratford Express,* 27 June 1885.

44. *Stratford Express,* 4 July 1885, Volckman lived at The White House. For Knotts Green see *VCH Essex,* vi. 179.

45. *Stratford Express,* 19 September 1885; 25 May 1895 (obit.). Worland had joined W Ham local board at the age of 23, became mayor of the county borough in 1890, but died at 41.

46. *Stratford Express,* 8 August 1885.

47. *Stratford Express,* 19 September, 17 October, 12 December 1885.

48. *Stratford Express,* 10 September 1887.

49. *VCH Essex,* vi. 219.

50. *Stratford Express,* 26 September 1885.

51. *Stratford Express,* 7 November 1885.

52. *Stratford Express,* 28 November 1885.

53. S A Shipley, *The Stratford Dialectical and Radical Club,* (unpublished thesis, Ruskin College, Oxford, 1967. Copy in Newham reference library). See also Stan Shipley, *Club Life and Socialism in Mid-Victorian London* (Ruskin College, *History Workshop* pamphlet No. 5, 1971).

54. For this school: *VCH Essex,* vi. 235.

55. For the SPEL: S Shipley, *Club Life and Socialism,* 69-70.

56. E P Thompson, *William Morris, Romantic to Revolutionary* (1955), 330.

57. S Shipley, *Club Life and Socialism,* Handbill of programme of SDRC for May and June 1882.

58. This league was probably identical with the "Working Men's Association for the Abolition of Foreign Sugar Bounties", which was one of the organisations run by Kelly and Samuel Peters. See also below.

59. For these refineries: *VCH Essex,* vi. 80.

60. VCH *Essex,* ii, 496.

61. J Saville, "Trade Union and Free Labour," in *Essays in Labour History,* eds A Briggs and J Saville (1960), 317 f.

62. *Stratford Express,* 27 August 1884.

63. S A Shipley, *The Stratford Dialectical and Radical Club;* E P Thompson, *op. cit.,* 327 n, 328, 330-332, 414, 500, 530, 746.

64. Last known reference: *Stratford Express,* 17 September 1887.

65. S A Shipley, *The Stratford Dialectical and Radical Club; Kelly's Dir. Essex,* (1874 to 1886).

66. See below.

67. *Stratford Express,* 10 January 1885 (advertisement).

68. *Stratford Express,* 17 January 1885 (report).

69. *Stratford Express,* 28 February 1885. In the 1885 general election Cowan was defeated at Whitechapel by the Liberal, Samuel Montagu, later Lord Swaythling: *McCalmont's Parliamentary Poll Book,* eds J Vincent and M Stenton (1971); *DNB,* Montagu, Sam. (1832-1911).

70. *Stratford Express,* 25 July 1885.

71. *Stratford Express,* 10, 17 October 1885.

72. *Stratford Express,* 24, 31 October, 28 November 1885.

73. *McCalmont's Parliamentary Poll Book.* It is notable that in 1885, when West Ham's population was nearing 200,000, the total number of those voting in both constituencies was only 13,791. At that period the electorate was restricted to male freeholders and householders.

74. *Stratford Express,* 17 July 1886: letter from M Fleming, honorary secretary, Irish registration committee.

75. *Stratford Express,* 12, 26, June; 3, 17 July 1886 (attack and criticism); 10 July 1886 (silly "Sodom and Gomorrah" speech).

76. *Stratford Express,* 17 April 1886.

77. *Stratford Express,* 8 May 1886.

78. *Stratford Express,* 12 December 1885.

79. *Stratford Express,* 12, 19 June 1886.

80. *Stratford Express,* 3 July 1886: comments by J Leicester on "the notorious Newman, Kelly and Peters gang".

81. *Stratford Express,* 26 June 1886.

82. *Stratford Express,* 3 July 1886.

83. *McCalmont's Parliamentary Poll Book; Stratford Express,* 10 July 1886.

84. *Stratford Express,* 7 July 1888.

85. *Stratford Express,* 2 July 1892.

86. *Stratford Express,* 17 August 1889.

87. *Stratford Express,* 31 August, 21 September 1889.

88. *Stratford Express,* 26 January 1889.

89. *Stratford Express,* 19 February 1887, 19 January 1889.

90. *Stratford Express,* 30 January 1892 (obit.); *DNB*: Hume, Joseph

91. *McCalmont's Parliamentary Poll Book.*

92. *Stratford Express,* 21 April 1888, Webster's account of the origin and progress of his candidature.

93. *Stratford Express,* 8 January 1887.

94. *Stratford Express,* 18 June 1887, Letter from Dr J Moir.

95. *Stratford Express,* 22 January 1887.

96. *Stratford Express,* 15 October 1887, Webster meeting, at which "unanimity prevailed".

97. *Stratford Express,* 5 February 1887. For Labouchere, Lawson, O'Connor and Arch see *DNB*. For Conybeare (1853-1919) see *Who was Who.*

98. *Stratford Express,* 29 January, 12 February, 5 March, 2 April, 14 May, 18 June, 16, 23 July 1887; 18 February 1888. Morgan was later said to be "a commission agent in the hat trade": *Stratford Express,* 17 October 1890.

99. *Stratford Express,* 6 August, 10, 17 September 1887.

100. *Stratford Express,* 7 December 1889: Alderman Henry Phillips.

101. *Stratford Express,* 10 December 1887: anonymous letter from "Nemo solus sapit".

102. *Stratford Express,* 21 April 1888.

103. *Stratford Express,* 21 May 1887; 12 May 1888; 22 October 1888.

104. *Stratford Express,* 20 December1890.

105. Calculated from *Stratford Express* reports, 1887-90.

106. *Stratford Express,* 19 May, 9 June 1888; 14 May, 10 August 1889; 5 December 1891.

107. *Stratford Express,* 26 January 1889.

108. *Stratford Express,* 25 April 1888.

109. *Stratford Express,* 11 August 1888.

110. *Stratford Express,* 28 April 1888.

111. *Stratford Express,* 21 April, 12 May 1888.

112. Foresters (*Stratford Express,* 9 June 1888); Ancient Britons (*Stratford Express,* 28 July 1888); Druids (*Stratford Express,* 22 June 1889); United Friends (*Stratford Express,* 21 June 1890); Sailors' and Firemen's Union (*Stratford Express,* 12 October 1889); V & A Dockers' Union (*Stratford Express,* 5 October 1889).

113. *Stratford Express,* 20 December 1890.

114. This paragraph is based on *Stratford Express,* August to October 1889.

115. *Stratford Express,* 18 August 1888.

116. *Stratford Express,* 16 February (cf. 2 February) 1889. Cremer (1838-1908), see *DNB*.

117. *Stratford Express,* 19 January 1889.

118. *Stratford Express,* 23 November 1889.

119. The borough council, formed in 1886, comprised 36 councillors and 12 aldermen.

120. *Stratford Express,* 7 December 1889.

121. *Stratford Express,* 7, 14 December 1889. Sir Henry Campbell-Bannerman was proposed as arbitrator.

122. *Stratford Express,* 4 January 1890.

123. For Sir Morell Mackenzie (1837-92) see *DNB*. His best known patient, the Emperor Frederick III of Germany, had died of throat cancer in 1888.

124. *Stratford Express,* 1 February 1890.

125. For Keir Hardie's early career see F Reid, *op. cit.*

126. For the Scottish Labour Party, its officers and programme, see *Stratford Express,* 14 May 1892. For Cunninghame Graham (1852-1936) see *DNB.*

127. F Reid, *op. cit.,* 128; *Stratford Express,* 18 June 1892.

128. *Stratford Express,* 19 April 1890.

129. *Stratford Express,* 26 April 1890, reporting meeting of 23 April. For Josiah Foster see *VCH Essex,* vi. 130.

130. *Stratford Express,* 17 May 1890.

131. F Reid, *op. cit.,* 128; *Stratford Express,* 31 January 1890. For Thorne (1857-1946) see *DNB.* He was later MP for West Ham South and mayor of West Ham.

132. *Stratford Express,* 7, 21 March, 18 April 1891.

133. *Stratford Express,* 21 March 1891.

134. *Stratford Express,* 4, 11, 18 July; 1, 22 August 1891.

135. *Stratford Express,* 5 December 1891.

136. *Stratford Express,* 5 December 1891.

137. *Stratford Express,* 16 January 1892.

138. *Stratford Express,* 30 January 1892.

139. *Stratford Express,* 23, 30 January 1892. For this "Russian flu" epidemic, in which the Duke of Clarence, Queen Victoria's grandson, died, see *Haydn's Dictionary of Dates* (1898 edn.), s.v. Influenza.

140. *Stratford Express,* 6 February 1892; *DNB.*

141. *Stratford Express,* 23 January 1892.

142. *Stratford Express,* 30 January 1892: the wreaths included "a very beautiful one ... from Miss Hall-Hall, with a pathetic message ... heart-shaped, made of costly arum lilies ... intertwined with cypress and bay". Her relationship to Webster is not known.

143. West Ham's official history, *Fifty Years a Borough,* ed. D McDougall (1936), mentions Hume Webster only once, without naming him (271).

144. *Stratford Express,* 6, 13, 20 February 1892.

145. *Stratford Express,* 13 February 1892.

146. *Stratford Express,* 2 April 1892. For Mansfield House see *VCH Essex,* vi. 142.

147. *Stratford Express,* 9 April 1892.

148. *Stratford Express,* 20 February, 16 April 1892.

149. *Stratford Express,* 23, 30 April 1892; F Reid, *op. cit.,* 130.

150. *Stratford Express,* 25 June 1892.

151. *Stratford Express,* 25 June, 2 July 1892.

152. *Stratford Express,* 2 July 1892.

153. BL, Add. MS 44295, f. 277, 7 July 1892.

154. National Liberal Club, Election Addresses 1892, West Ham South.

155. *Stratford Express,* 23 April 1892.

156. *Stratford Express,* 9 July 1892.

157. *ibid.*

158. *Stratford Express,* 23 July 1892. Among other subscribers were William Saunders, MP for Newington, Walworth, W S Caine, MP for Bradford East, the Dockers' Union, and J S Curwen. A later statement gives the total as £297: *Stratford Express,* 13 August 1892. See also: F Reid, *op. cit.,* 137f

159. *Stratford Express,* 8 October 1892; 11 February, 19, 26 August, 16 September, 16 December 1893; 22 December 1894; 9, 23 February; 2, 16 March 1895; F Reid, *op. cit.,* 156f.

160. *Stratford Express,* 22 December 1894.

161. *Stratford Express,* 9 February 1895.

162. *Stratford Express,* 23 February, 2, 16 March, 1895.

163. F Reid, *op. cit.,* 136; *Stratford Express,* 13, 27 August, 1892.

164. *Stratford Express,* 15 October 1892.

165. *Stratford Express,* 22 October 1892.

166. *Stratford Express,* 14 April 1894.

167. *Stratford Express,* 30 June 1894.

168. *Stratford Express,* 12 May 1894.

169. *Stratford Express,* 27 October, 29 December 1894.

170. *Stratford Express,* 29 June 1895.

171. *Stratford Express,* 20 July 1895. For Ring see *Kelly's Dir. Essex* (1892) s.v. Silvertown.

172. *Stratford Express,* 17 August 1895.

173. *Stratford Express,* 7 December 1895. At Mansfield House.

174. Will Thorne, who had opposed Banes in 1900, won West Ham (South) in 1906. He held it until 1918 when the constituency was split into two. From 1918 until his retirement in 1945 he was MP for the West Ham, Plaistow division.

175. A friend tells me that her grandparents, strong Labour supporters in West Ham, always had a picture of Keir Hardie in their living room.

Index

Fabian Society, 2
Fielding, John, 2
Fleming, M (Irish Registration Committee) note 74
Foote, G W, atheist, 6
Foster, Josiah, Baptist minister, 17
Frederick III, Emperor of Germany (d. 1888), note 123
Freedom, anarchist journal, 11
Freiheit Defence Committee, 10
Fulcher, Cllr Edward (L), 6, 14, 19

Gascoyne-Cecil, Robert, Marquis of Salisbury (C), Prime Minister, 5, 12
Given-Wilson, Thomas, vicar of Plaistow, 9
Gladstone, William E (L), Prime Minister, 12, 19
Godstone (Surrey), see Marden Park
Gould, Philip, 4
Graham, Robert B Cunninghame MP (L), 17
Gray, Matthew, (L), rubber manufacturer, note 29
Great Eastern Railway works, Stratford, 5
Grove, Archibald, MP (L), 20

Hainault Forest, note 4
Hall-Hall, Miss, note 142
Ham, East, 3
Ham, West, Artillery volunteers, 5; borough cllrs, 13-14, 16, 18-10; Canning Town, 5,
    7-9, 13-17, 19-20, 22; local board, 5; Plaistow, 5-7, 9, 12, 16; school board, 5-6;
    Silvertown, 10, 22; Stratford, 5-7, 9-11, 20; Tidal Basin, 11, 15, 19; Trades
    Council, 20
Hampstead, London, 2
Hardie, James Keir MP (Labour), 2-5, 17-22
Hatfield Forest, note 4.
High, Richard (L), 14
Howard, David (C), chemical manufacturer, 5
Hume, Joseph, MP (L), 13
Hyndman, Henry M, SDF leader, 10

Independent Labour Party, 2
Irish, electors, 12, 16, 21-22; Home Rule, 4, 5, 12, 17, 19-20, 22

Johnston, Andrew, note 27

Keating, J Ledger, secretary to Hume Webster, 16
Kelly, Thomas, bogus trade union leader, 10-12. For his "gang" see Lemon, Tom;
    McLean, John; Newman, Edwin; Peters, Samuel.

Kennington, London, 2
Kropotkin, Prince Pëtr, Russian revolutionary, 10

Labouchere, Henry, MP (L), 14; Mrs Henry (L), 15
Lambeth (London), 8
Lanarkshire, Mid., parl. const., 17; NW, parl. const., 17
Lawson, Sir Wilfrid, MP (L), 14
Leicester, Joseph, MP (L), 7-9, 12-13, 19, 21
Lemon, "Captain" Tom, 10-12. See also Kelly, Thomas.
Leyton (Essex), 15; Church Rd. board school, 10; Knotts Green, 8
London, 2-3, 5, 10, 13-14; Chamber of Commerce, 11; Co-operative Society, 4; sheriff,
    11. See also Lambeth

Mackenzie, Sir Morell, physician, 17-18
McLean, John, 11. See also Kelly, Thomas
Makins, William, MP (C), 5
Marden Park, in Godstone (Surrey), 13, 15, 18
Marx, Eleanor, note 20
"Match girls'" strike, 1888, 4
Maudsley, James, (C) cotton workers' leader, 2
Moir, Dr John, (L), 5, 14, 17; note 33
Montagu, Samuel, Lord Swaythling, note 69
Montrose (Forfar, Scotland), 13
Morgan, William (L), 14
Morley, Arnold, MP (L), 16-17; John, MP (L), later Viscount Morley, 21-22
Most, Johann, German revolutionary, 10

National Reformer, radical magazine, 10
National Secular Society, 6, 10
Newcastle-upon-Tyne, MP for (L), 21-22
Newman, Edwin, 12. See also Kelly, Thomas.
Nonconformists, 5, 14, 16-17, 21
Northampton, MP for, 14

O'Connor, Thomas P, MP (L), 14, 17
Oldham, 2

Paris (France), 8
Pearce, William (C), 12
Peters, Samuel, bogus trade unionist, 10-12. See also Kelly, Thomas.
Phillips, Alderman Henry (L), 16, 19
Pittsburgh (Penn., USA), 20
Pound, Alfred J (C), 12
Primrose, Archibald, Earl of Rosebery, Prime Minister, 20

Primrose League (C), 12

Radical magazine, 10
Radical Alliance Club, Stratford, 9
Reeves, Hugh (L agent), 14
Ring, Timothy, Roman Catholic priest, 22
Rochdale Pioneers, 3
Roman Catholics, 16, 22
Ronan, James (L), 11
Rosebery, Earl of, see Primrose, Archibald.

Salisbury, Marquis of, see Gascoyne-Cecil, Robert.
Saunders, William, MP, note 158
Savill, Philip (C), brewer, 5
Schnadhorst, Francis (L agent), 5, 19
Scotland, 2, 18. See also Montrose
Scottish Labour Party, 2, 5, 17
Seamen's Society, 11
Shoreditch, Haggerston, MP for (L), 16
Smith, W H (L), 7-8, 13-14
Social Democratic Federation, 2-3, 9-10
Socialist League, 2, 9
Social and Political Education League, 10
Stratford Co-operative Society, 3
Stratford Dialectical and Radical club, 4, 10-11
Stratford Express, 21; notes, *passim*
Sugar Operatives Society, 11
Sugar refining, 10-12
Swaythling, Lord, see Montagu, Samuel.

Temperance reform, 5, 7, 14, 17, 20
Thorne, Cllr William J, later MP (Labour), 3-4, 18
Tillett, Ben (ILP), 2
Tower Hamlets, Whitechapel constituency, 12

Volckman, Mrs Elizabeth (L), 8; William (L), 6-9, 14

Walsh, John (L), 18; Cllr Thomas (L), 19
Walthamstow (Essex), 15
Webster, James Hume (L), 13-19; Mrs Hume, 15; Miss Hume, 15; Noel Hume, 15
West Ham Central Liberal Association, 13
West Ham Liberal Association, 5
West Ham North, constituency, 5, 7-8, 11-12, 20
Williams, Jack (SDF), 2

THE SOCIALIST HISTORY SOCIETY

The Socialist History Society was founded in 1992 and includes many leading Socialist and labour historians in Britain and overseas. We have a growing membership of both academic and amateur historians. The SHS holds regular events, public meetings and one-off conferences, and contributes to current historical debates and controversies. The society produces a range of publications, including the journal *Socialist History*. We can sometimes assist with individual student research.

The SHS is the successor to the Communist Party History Group, established in 1946. The society is now independent of all political parties and groups. We are engaged in and seek to encourage historical studies from a Marxist and broadly-defined left perspective. We are concerned with every aspect of human history from early social formations to the present day and aim for a global reach. We are particularly interested in the struggles of labour, women, progressive and peace movements throughout the world, as well as the movements and achievements of colonial peoples, black people, and other oppressed communities in seeking justice, human dignity and liberation.

Each year we produce two issues of our journal *Socialist History*, one or two historical pamphlets in our *Occasional Papers* series, and members' newsletters.

We hold a public lecture and debate in London five times per year. In addition, we organise occasional conferences, book-launch meetings, and joint events with other sympathetic groups. We aim to hold more events outside London.

Join the Socialist History Society!
Members receive all our serial publications for the year at no extra cost and regular mailings about our activities. Members can vote at our January AGM and seek election to positions on the committee. Members are encouraged to participate in other ways.

Annual membership fees due January each year:

Full UK	£20.00
Concessionary UK	£14.00
Overseas full	£25.00
Overseas concessionary	£19.00

To join, please send your name and address plus a cheque/PO payable to **Socialist History Society** to: The Secretary, SHS, 50 Elmfield Road, Balham, London SW17 8AL.

Visit our website on http://www.socialisthistorysociety.co.uk